Not For Everybody

This poetry collection represents a celebration of our six
mental faculties - intuition, imagination, perception, reason,
will and memory.

Vicky Boulton

ISBN 978-1-78792-051-4

Book design, layout and production management by Into Print
www.intoprint.net

+44 (0)1604 832149

"I am not for everyone. I know my truth, I know who I am, I know what I do and do not bring to the table. I'm not easy to deal with, but I do bring tons of value. I bring love and strength, but I am not perfect, and if I don't fit in with a person, or group, that is okay with me."

- Sylvester McNutt

Contents

Connections

Guilt

It's a tightrope between feeling suffocated by your needs,
Or weighed down by the heavy burden of guilt.

Some days it's too much and I want to run away and hide.
Ignore you and live my own life,
Where instead of using me as a verbal punchbag,
You will step up, make good decisions and own your situation,
With all its intricacies and complexities.

Who knows, if that ever happens,
You might feel able to fight your own battles -
Leaving me free to pursue my future
With you no longer pulling the strings.

Different

She knew she was different before she understood why.
Always sensed something,
Realised things didn't add up,
But didn't grasp what it meant.

Years later, in possession of all the facts,
Nothing really changed.
Other than knowing she was special – in a good way.
    Chosen.
        Wanted.
            Given so much by those
                Whose features she would never inherit,
                    But whose love was beyond question.

The Secret of Us

Sometimes there's so much to say.
Not enough moments to process everything.
Words come out too quickly
Rushed and not always right
Leading to true meanings becoming lost.

Other times there's nothing to say.
Long pauses persist.
Silence abounds.
Time to hear what's not been said.
Space to think, understand, reflect and plan.

And so, begins a pattern.
Throughout each day, week, month and year
We sit together in noise and quiet.
Eager to talk and share.
Happy to listen.

A sort of shared formula.
Vital pieces that fit –

The secret of us
Bit by bit.

Ghosted

No option. No say. No way to change the course -
Can't influence the outcome, track the poison to its source.

Messages remain unanswered, so much left unsaid -
I was never even consulted, met with stony silence instead.

One day you just decided, our friendship was complete -
That it was time to move on and happily pressed *'delete.'*

I think I want answers, need you to call up and share -
Understand the hurt I'm feeling, make you fully aware.

I thought ghosting happened to others, not people like you and me,
Just shows I am wrong and how elusive you're proving to be.

Knew

I thought I knew everything about you.
Every emotion.
Thought.
Gesture.
I was mistaken.

On that day I witnessed something.
Saw you differently through unaccustomed eyes.
The way you sought him out.
Lingering looks,
Loving words,
Intimate touches.
The fact you just fitted together.
The absolute rawness of human love
Was magical.
Fairy tale like.
Stuff that childhood dreams are made of.
I felt like an intruder -
Empty-handed,
With no treasure of my own.

But I was glad my friend,
        Happy you can finally now say
                'I've found it and I'm not
                Ever letting it get away.'

'Busy'

Instead of telling me, and your other so-called friends online,
How busy you are and how short of time you are
Why don't you just get on quietly and do what needs to be done
Without inviting:
        sympathy,
        encouragement,
        support
        and perhaps most importantly, validation?

After all, being busy is not exactly something new.
Some of us have been dealing with the concept forever,
Many single handedly, smashing it on a daily basis,
Without feeling the need to
        utter
        a
        single
        word.

She Said

She said I invested more in my friends
Because I *'didn't have any children.'*
I don't think she meant to be cruel,
Hope she was just being honest,
Shame she wasn't better informed.

I invest in my friends because of what they do for me.
How they make me feel.
How we help each other.
How they are there for me... no matter what.

Because that's how precious great friendships are.
Carefully chosen people, whom I love without question.
And who I would willingly run through fire to save,
Even if it means getting burnt along the way.

Playing The Game

To get on in life you must
   Follow the rules,
      Do as you are told
         Accept the status quo
         Try to fit in.

Except I don't.
Superficially perhaps.
Half-heartedly certainly -
Just enough to fool them:
   Convince others of my credentials.
   Pull the wool over their eyes.
      Let them believe I am one of them.
      Make them trust me.
         Never suspect my motives,
         Or question my integrity.

But then you came along.
How easily you saw through '*me*'!
Recognised a kindred spirit.
   Someone who could be useful.
      Whose cover you might share.

And I was so grateful for having you here,
      Celebrating our differences, year after year,
         As we let them believe we are just the same,
         Willing participants in this never-ending game.

15

Dignified

And those gathered neither mourned nor cried.
Her life had meant so little, that her death gave no reason,
For anything more elaborate.

Her friendship I had lost through doubt and fear.
Call it cowardice, or weakness, but to me she had changed.
She tried to explain.
I turned away.
Her company no longer held any realistic charms.

Afraid of her unstable moods, I watched the decline.
Her fall from society and she so oblivious to it.
A woman so keen to forget herself.
Desperately lonely, or desperate to be alone?

I could never have helped her. My last duty is today,
Watching her laid to rest, so peaceful and dignified
That I could have cried, had I not known what
Had killed her... willingly it seemed
And separated us forever.

Layers

She's my rock, my confidante.
Witness to every disaster, or triumph.
The person I want to share
My thoughts, dreams and plans with.
Someone I trust never to let me down,
Or try to change me.

I love her to the ends of the earth and back.
Enjoy spending time with her,
As we go over the same old ground
Happy to let each other see
What lies behind our world-ready faces.

Daily we expose the rawness beneath.
Showcase vulnerabilities.
Share lost hopes, unrealised dreams
Trade secrets, stories and experiences.
All the time looking for similarities,
Connections, empathy, or just permission
To peel back yet another layer.
Reveal the one behind the mask
Who is beautifully flawed,
but mercifully unburdened
And is content to sit comfortably beside me -
Whatever the weather... and be my friend forever.

connections

Worth

Naval Gazing

Holding up a mirror to yourself is tough.
There are parts I don't like.
Add a tangle of suppressed emotions,
Learnt behaviours, outdated views.
It's a wonder I've survived so long.

Amazing to think that all this time I struggled for perfection,
Saw weakness in others as an opportunity to shine brighter,
I was wrong.
About that.
About everything.
Especially when it came to me.

How dare I sit in judgement on others,
Allow myself to also be judged
And let others decide my worth.
What's the point?
Where's it got me?

When faced with my own hang-ups, imperfections
And mistakes, how easy is it to lash out,
Blame someone else.
Point fingers at people, situations and events.
Shirk responsibility and look for excuses?

But how much more grown-up
To take ownership, accept you're human?
Look disappointment in the eye and acknowledge
You're willing to take the time to heal yourself
From the inside out.

Making it Happen

Tickets not booked.
Museums left unvisited.
Trips awaiting payment.
Reservations left unconfirmed.
Invitations never sent.
Holidays remain untaken.
Restaurant tables empty.
Birthday cards unsigned.
Gifts stay unbought.
Thank yous unsaid.

So if you think I'm superfluous
With tasks any idiot can do.
Let's see what happens,
When it's all left up to you?

Currency

I don't care what gender you are,
Am not bothered by your pronouns,
What injustices you are fighting,
The colour of your skin,
Your preferred safe space,
If you're in a wheelchair,
Or struggling to control your demons.
My only request is that if you can be just one thing
Please choose to be kind.
Because kindness is a currency
That will always be valued.

Forgiveness

Be proud of who you are and everything you've achieved.
Stop stressing at what you've still got left to do.
Refrain from building obstacles you feel you must overcome.
Give up shelving your needs and dreams for others.
Call *'time'* on needing to rescue friends and family.

If you must do something.
Try sitting still and simply breathing.
In… and… out…
Release pain, disappointment,
Frustration and doubt.
Offer beautiful thoughts a home and
Look for happiness in the smallest of things.

But above all:
Be kind and forgive yourself.
See the truth and embrace its simplicity -
You might not be perfect, but you are a good person.
And the daily punishments you continue to inflict on yourself
Do not fit any crime you believe you might have committed.

That

At various time of our lives
We are all a little bit...
   broken
        confused
           let down
   imperfect
                disappointed
       frustrated
          sad
  lost
         disillusioned
     pained   grief-stricken

The secret is to keep these parts separate.

Acknowledge them if you must.
But don't let them determine who you are,
Or rule your life.

You are worth so much more than each of these emotions -
Either separately or collectively.

Each one marks a time, a place or a situation
Where you stumbled, but didn't give up.
So, if you must let something define you...
Let it be that.

No Reprieve

Foolishly she hoped you'd change,
Realise her worth before she slipped through your hands.
Appreciate everything she had given you,
Cherish years of precious memories,
Not only listened to her advice,
But also chosen to take it.

Perhaps if you had correctly understood her words,
Spent more time interpreting their meaning,
Been aware of her stark and final warning,
You wouldn't be here.
Stuttering for an answer.
Hoping for a reprieve.
Praying for a final chance,
As my brave, bold and brilliant friend
Calls you out one last time.

Chocolate

I believed her when she said she'd had it rough.
And all the chocolate in the world wasn't enough,
To compensate for everything she had endured.
With feelings and emotions left unsecured.
By those who wanted more, but just got less
From a wicked child who failed to impress.

I asked her what would make it right,
Release her mind, leave her feeling light.
She paused a moment to consider her choice
Acknowledging the novelty of having a voice.
'Love' she said, that would be a good start,
So, without hesitation, I gave her my heart.

Brightness

I feel for people who have so little self-belief and confidence
That instead of blazing their own unique trail through life,
They hitch their ambitions and dreams to someone else
    – Usually a brighter star –
        And then seem content to follow in their wake forever
        Never once questioning if the direction in which they
        Are heading, is actually where they want to go.

All Along

What if I was mistaken?
Everything was a lie.
Feelings confused,
Completely misinterpreted
He had never loved me.
Couldn't be that brave
To take a stand…
Even for me, for us.

What if things were different?
Wrongly remembered.
Imaginations flawed,
Appetites suppressed
Desire replaced by indifference.
Apologies few… if any
I guess worse than all these things…
Is if you were right all along.

Copycat

When did you last have an original thought
Freely proffer a personal opinion - out loud
Make your own decision and stick to it
No matter what happened.

When did you last switch off your phone
Mute the noise, avoid liking, commenting
Or sharing stories that you never proved
Were honest, kind or true.

When did you last have the confidence
To say no, this is not for me
I don't want to be involved
I need to do things my way.

When did you last watch, read, or buy
Something that wasn't recommended
By those paid to influence you
Thus removing any free choice.

When did you last take the time
To live in the moment, be grateful
Know your own worth
And refuse to be judged
For not following the crowd?

Artificial

You said that since I left,
Everything had fallen apart.
You cited my cruelty
And disregard for your feelings.
How you had ended up alone.
Broken. Half the man you were.
Bruised, battered and adrift.

Warming to the subject matter,
You told me you couldn't bring yourself
To do the things we used to
Including looking after our plants -
Talking to them was no longer appropriate
Whilst watering them was a step too far.
You said they had died, like our love
And that was all on me.

Shame, I declared, because those plants
You claim I wilfully abandoned,
Without a thought for their welfare
Were actually plastic
And as artificial
As your self-made drama
And the couple we used to be.

Let Go

She never deserved you,
Your love, trust, patience and loyalty.
She took from you
Time and time again - and you let her
Believing that was the deal, never once
Questioned if you could ask for more.

It could have gone on like that forever.
This all-encompassing relationship
That you clung to.
Fearful of losing someone
Who understood who you were
And more importantly where you came from.

But then something changed and it made you look -
Closely and deeply into whether this
Friendship still served you well.
And when the answer came back, you were confused,
Hurt, then angry; more at yourself than her,
Because you should have put a stop to it years ago
Although you never did –
Partly because of your steadfast loyalty,
But mainly because you thought it was okay
To give more than to receive and to prioritise
Someone else's needs above your own.

worth

Understanding

Taking Part

You're my weakness.
Achilles heel.
Fly in the ointment.
Bane of my life.
Because you know
> Too much
> What buttons to press...
> And when.

> You push. I react.
> Together we spar like amateur boxers
> Who've learnt the moves,
> But can't close it out.

> Back and forth we go,
> Scoring points as we trade blows,
> Wanting to hurt each other,
> Display strength.
> Be seen as the best.

This exchange is well practised.
Fruitless hours spent fighting
For one-upmanship.
But the satisfaction of wiping that smile
Off your smug, familiar face
Is sometimes all that keeps me going.

But what's the point? Why bother?
When we both know that in reality,
The taking part is everything,
Because there can never be a winner.

Not For Everybody

Two non-negotiable facts.
You won't like everyone
And not everyone will like you.

Every person has their own preferences, opinions, and
Experiences which shape how they perceive others.
It's important to focus on being true to yourself -
Invest in authenticity and individuality; be real.

Refuse to pander to the whim of others;
Don't change your behaviours
To win approval, or measure your worth
By yielding to unrealistic
And lofty expectations.
Stop trying so hard to fit in;
Save your energy for those who *get* you
– First time - with no explanation needed.

By surrounding yourself with people
Who appreciate you for who you are
And who you love and feel comfortable with,
You'll find it easier to accept that you are not for everybody.
Your unique brilliance has a special audience and
The truth of this knowledge is all you need to know.

Blue Lights

There are two distinct types of people in the world.
The one who when driving and confronted by an ambulance
En route to the hospital, with blue lights flashing
And sirens wailing,
Moves quickly to the side of the road - minimal fuss
And is thankful it's someone else inside and not them.

The other kind moans.
Takes their time.
Resents giving way.
Questions driving standards.
And has too much to say about their inconvenience.

I always knew which one I was,
But until today,
I had only guessed - wrongly it seems - about you.

I See You

Don't worry… I know you're here.
Can feel your presence,
That particular type of energy you bring,
Forceful. Pushy. Impatient.

But although I see you,
Don't expect me to react.
I've wised up to your drama.
Learnt not to be taken in,
Manipulated and primed.

I won't hang onto every word,
Be another pet project.
Believe what you tell me.
Ignore others to be available.

You've never really valued me.
I'm worth more than you'll ever know.
And if I can keep you at arm's length -
            Free from your need to change me
                    Into that person you want me to be -
                        I will be okay.

Power

You didn't break me; you don't have that kind of power.
You just bruised me temporarily.
Made me stop and realise that
For too long I've been blinded to your faults,
Ignored the voices in my head
Telling me that you're not good enough for me -
That we're done.

But now I'm listening,
Seeing and realising
   How much sweeter is the silence
   How much stronger is my will
   How much better I can be
      Without you and your criticisms
      Your need to control me
      And your thinly veiled disappointment
         Which I now realise stems
         From your, rather than my own, failings.

Unwanted Guests

Date agreed.
Invitations sent.
Catering confirmed.
Bar set up and ready.

Only a select gathering - just five guests in all -
Shame, Guilt, Expectation, Duty and Responsibility.
All here to remind you what you
Should
Could
And must do.

At this pity party, there are no victors,
Just a sense of anger and disbelief.
A timely reminder of what you've lost
By sticking to unspoken rules,
Observing suffocating boundaries,
Displaying behaviours that were taught as a child.
And which have been unconsciously reinforced
Every single day
Until they became your own uneasy truth.
Forcing you to repeat others' mistakes.
And preventing you from moving forwards.

To Be Honest

People say they want it, need it,
Cite its loss as part of the problems
We all now face in our lives.
Yet when questioned, some admit they can't always handle it,
Would rather a toned-down, filtered version,
Generally something more pleasing and kind.
Which is why, when invited to share my opinion, or thoughts,
I clarify if others want me to be completely candid,
Share truthful information and not distort any facts.
And I've long since stopped being surprised
By how few actually say 'Yes.'

Empty

Don't you get sick of smiling?
Of saying the right things.
Being accommodating.
Flexible.
Obliging.
Pleased to help.
Keen to be included.
Happy for others.
Needing to feel involved,
Important - no matter how insignificant your role?

I do.
I find it exhausting.
Investing all that precious energy
In trying to secure someone else's happiness,
Whilst all the time my own tank
Dips dangerously into empty.

Squander

What a waste!

Wanting to be: Thinner?
Prettier?
Cooler?
Smarter?
Funnier?
Fitter?
Healthier?
Better?

All that unrealistic perfection,
Tempting you to change
And which even now continues to allude you.

How negligent!

All those years spent trying to be someone else
Instead of taking the time to appreciate
The quirky amazingness that is you.

Groundhog Day

If life's a learning curve
Why do we repeat familiar mistakes,
Not once, but again and again?

Like the time you told me it was over.
I begged for a change of heart, with no pride
Integrity, or sense of my own worth,
Until you gave in.

But the die was cast.

We ended as I knew we must

    Bitterly
        Painfully
            Sadly

But even the cold light of day
Hasn't stopped me from wondering
Whether the outcome would be different if we tried again...

Shape of Pain

You don't make it easy.
Think nothing of adding extra hurdles
At the last minute.
Anything to trip me up,
Push me into the usual
Ocean of guilt
Where I'm the villain -
The baddie of the piece.
Someone who should behave better,
Correctly interpret the silence
Take time to solve the problem
And hang around until the bitter end.
It's impossible to challenge this status quo
Thanks to established family dynamics
That continue to rise unashamed
Remind me who I am and
Seek to bring me down…

One

More

Time.

Tiny Moments

It's not one big thing booked and delivered
In a timely fashion on special occasions.

Instead it's hundreds of tiny moments
Designed to surprise and delight you.

> A stranger's kind look
> A big slice of cake
> A beautiful sunset
> A friend's giggle
> A host of daffodils
> A heartfelt compliment
> A new dress
> A brilliant film
> Or an engrossing book
> Where the meaning stays with you
> Making you smile.

Joy does not wait for a summons,
Or strictly adhere to certain times.
Instead you must seek it out
In your surroundings, circumstances,
Via people, places and through chance.
Stop to take the time to appreciate
Its worth in simple actions and gestures.

But when you do discover it
- No matter how small or insignificant it may seem -
Remember to practise gratitude and contentment.
Only then will you truly understand
That it's the little things that matter, not the big stuff,
Because joy is a fraction; something we must experience
Every single day for just a chance to feel whole.

understanding

Words

Good Enough

Is it finished yet, you asked,
Or have you more to do?
Are you pleased with what you've written,
Or will you add in something new?

Is it finished yet, you asked,
Or has an emotion not been conveyed,
As precisely as it needs to be -
Meaning your progress is delayed?

Is it finished yet, you asked,
Or are you mid artistic flow?
Could you possibly take a break,
Or is creativity green for go?

Is it finished yet, you asked,
Or are you struggling with a word
That will resonate with your readers -
Ensuring your brilliance is heard?

Is it finished yet, you asked,
Or should more attention be paid,
As you wrestle with a couplet,
Meaning supper is delayed.

Is it finished yet, you asked,
Surely there's nothing more say -
We need to talk about us
But your poetry's in the way

It's finished now, I said,
Please don't get in such a huff.
It definitely isn't perfect
But I think it's good enough.

Same Page

I wrote a poem.
It was about the frustrations of love
And the finality of choice,
Neatly capturing a place where I used to be.

A colleague read the same words.
They made her feel empowered,
Willing to take on the world,
Eager to make her mark.

A friend read the same words.
They made her feel sad,
Evoking emotions of a time before,
That she wanted to forget.

When you read the same words.
You said you felt nothing,
Were unmoved by the syllables,
The rhythm or meaning.

Were you trying to be awkward,
Or was it because you knew,
That those significant words
Were written about you?

Number Two

I love reading poetry whilst sitting upon the loo.
Sometimes for a number one, mostly it's a number two.
You get such peace and quiet upon a porcelain throne.
Time to read aloud, in the safety of your own home.

Some poets just work better, it's important to say,
Chirpy lines and stanzas, nothing too heavy in the way -
Brian Bilston and Sophie Hannah, followed by Wendy Cope -
Relevant, clever and humorous, brim-filled with tittering hope.

I once attempted Philip Larkin and some early Thom Gunn
Too much raw and honest emotion, definitely lacking in fun.
There was a dalliance with Dickinson, an encounter with Poe
Obviously very literary, but still mind-numbingly slow.

So I stick with the ones, where the meaning is quite clear
Pam Ayres, Carol Ann Duffy and Edward Lear.
Their rhyming is so pleasing, in fact an awesome job
All very acceptable when you're not a poetry snob.

Last Word

I used to want to make a mark.
An indelible memory.
A great impression.
Leave people reeling by scathing one-liners.
Stunned by my witty repartee.
Floored by a closing sarcastic remark.
I had to have the last word, text or message
My insecurities told me it mattered –
Completely wrongly, or so it seems.

These days I don't care at all.
Rather than delivering a sucker punch finale.
I prefer to keep people hanging,
Waiting impatiently.
Occasionally I forget to respond at all,
Leave conversations unfinished,
Meanings set adrift for days.

The longer it continues,
The less I mind.
And it's this feeling that's so surprising
As I wrap it firmly around me,
Take comfort in the discovery.
Wondering why for the first time in my life
It feels like I've come home?

Half a Job

I wrote half a poem
Not because I ran out of inspiration,
But because I wanted you as the reader to

>Process your feelings
>Stir some emotions
>Share experiences
>Find connections
>Realise possibilities
>Discover opportunities
>Value the world
>Relate to others better
>Understand human vulnerabilities
>Learn to appreciate language

I'm not being lazy
My words are subjective…
>True
>Lies
>Controversial
>Undisputed

It's your role to add another layer.
Provide a new voice.
Fill in the blanks.
Tell your own story.
Complete the poem.
Using your own words.
In your own inimitable style.

Missing in Action

I can't remember what I was saying...
Or the word -
You know the one
What do we use to wash up with?
Not dishcloth.
The other one?
Do you remember what we watched last night?
The 80's film with the actor we love -
Whose face I can picture, but that's it.
Lost along with so many other things like

Names
Birthdays
Dates
Car keys
Places
Mobile phones
Shopping lists
And invoices.

But it's words I miss most.
Nouns, verbs and adjectives -
All literally missing in action.
Unreachable, unmemorable, unrecallable -
Their importance as the building blocks of communication
Is not lost on anyone… especially me,
As conversations become stilted,
Empty, nonsensical and frustrating.
Another day passes,

Yet another favourite
Combination of significant letters
Opt out and remove themselves,
Albeit temporarily,
From my
   rapidly
        diminishing
           vocabulary.

Truth or Hyperbole?

She said she was so hungry; she could eat a horse.
Was literally dying of laughter
Could run faster than the wind
And she loved me to the moon and back.
She claimed she'd told me a million times
What really happened -
How she was not to blame, that lies were for fools.
She pleaded until the seas ran dry
And the sun scorched the earth.
I said I'd wait a lifetime for her -
She said it might take even longer.

Free

You wanted an argument.
An opportunity to be vocal,
State your views. Be controversial,
Or should that just read... right?
But when you picked on my poem,
Accused it of it not rhyming, or scanning,
Disputed its very core of existence
Questioned the subject, its meaning and flow,
You showed your ignorance... once again.

Because poems can shrug off conventions.
Be proud of themselves.
Happy in any construction,
Without need to conform
To the predictability of rhyme.
Instead, they can be open,
Only guilty of being free. –
And given your pedantic pettiness
That's a jolly lovely thing to be -
Just a shame you can't agree.

Alternative

If you feel the need to criticise,
Because you think you know better.
If you want to object loudly,
With the aim of putting someone down,
Or demonstrating your cleverness, wit and power,
I advise you to reconsider.

Instead of lashing out,
Take a moment and think.
Put yourself in their shoes -
Reassess.

Are your words helpful and constructive,
Or will they cause suffering and pain?
If they're going to do the latter
Then I urge you to kindly REFRAIN.

Sleepyhead

3am and I'm wide awake, thanks to
The many thoughts buzzing in my head,
Each fighting to be the first,
The most important and, of course, remembered.

Even in my drowsy state
I feel I owe it to them to try
To make sense of the jumble.
Craft words into an order.
Find a meaning that may resonate
With others like me.
Who might not appreciate structure,
Layout, rhyme and meter.
But instead want poems to console, comfort
And communicate a message.

I don't promise perfection -
That's the professional poet's domain -
Not for those who are sleep deprived
But eager to offer some precious words
So you know how you make me feel.

Little White Lies

Every day, they trip off your tongue -
Well-practised and inoffensive.
One for every occasion.
Words to fill the silence
Take the pressure off,
Prove you care and
Are worthy of being part of a relationship-
Whether that's family, friendship or work.
Does it matter what colour they are
- They're still lies.

But today as you trot out a few favourites…
    It's lovely to see you!
        We must do it again!
            I never got your message.
                I'll call you later.
                    I really enjoyed it!
                There's nothing's wrong.
        I'm fine!
    I honestly don't mind!
I love you.
They seem more barefaced than ever before
And I'm surprised he hasn't called you out on them,
Because I know, all too well, if the roles were reversed…
You would.

Decisions

Rewriting History

What are you doing here, standing in front of me shouting?
Demanding answers: eager to intimidate me
Just like you did 25 years ago
The last time I saw you.
The day you laid bare your threats,
Made clear the need for my absolute silence
And to operate according to your specific rules.

But now as I zone you out, ignore your histrionics,
I can see the years haven't been kind.
But for your eyes, arrogant smirk and your unbridled anger,
I would struggle to reconcile the two versions.
Recent events have heightened your paranoia,
Making you believe your behaviour is acceptable.
Whilst old age has swamped you in its embrace,
Causing your aggression to seem even more cruel.

But no matter how loud you shout,
Or the number of threats you make
I will never tell you where he is,
Or put you both in contact.
I can't believe you've forgotten so much –
Like how far I will go to protect those I love
From people who seek to rewrite history
To prove they weren't always wrong.

Failed Delivery

At night I can sense them.
I know they are there.
The promises, wishes, hopes
And every single dream I ever had,
Gather at the foot of my bed
Demanding to know
   What happened?
       Why they're unfulfilled?
          Whether it's too late?
             Why I let them down?
   And how they can staunch their hunger for the life
   I offered them,

       Then so cruelly failed to deliver.

Thanks...But

Not going to.
    Won't be joining you.
        Shan't make it.
            Can't face them.
                Don't want to be bothered.

When all's said and done,
    I'd rather stay here,
        Give the evening a miss.

And before you ask.
    It's nothing to do with you
        For once...
            It really is all about me.

Best

That dress that's hanging in your wardrobe.
Those impractical, but beautiful shoes.
The special bottle of champagne.
Expensive glasses, or crockery.
Voucher for a massage.
And all that other stuff you collect.
Why are they still unused, unworn and not yet enjoyed?

What are you waiting for?
A sign, a signal, a time when the stars align?
Whilst saving the good stuff for best is a great concept,
In reality will it ever happen?
My advice is to tell yourself that today
Is the right time and just dive in,
That way, you'll always have the best
When you least expect, but deserve it most.

What Could Have Been

I try not to think of what could have been.
I don't allow myself to speculate on the what ifs.
But occasionally when sleep alludes me,
You filter slowly into my brain.

Emails, messages or a call were never options
That would have worked for you.
So, instead I allow myself a moment to dwell
In a fantasy world of my own making.

Of course, we are still together.
Of course, we are sublimely happy.
Of course, everything is perfect.
Of course, this is all nonsense.

You are miles away with your family,
Taking every day as it comes.
Figuring out how to do your best
For those who you now love.

That's why I know with great certainty
That you could never be so weak or foolish,
To allow your thoughts to linger for even one second
On the us that might once have been.

Freedom

It's probably long overdue.
Completely obvious to everyone else.
But today I learnt a valuable lesson.

It's okay not to be good at things.
Perfectly acceptable not to push yourself to the limit,
To breaking point
A place where pain and sadness meet
And where giving up
Seems a sensible option.

Today I learnt it's okay to sit this one out.
Say I can't. I won't. It doesn't matter.
I don't care. I don't want it.

This knowledge changes everything.
Removes barriers which once made me stumble,
Question my abilities
My sanity, my strength
Brought me to my knees
And made me cry.

So today things are different.
Today it's okay to let go.
Put myself first
Do what I want
And be happy.

Find a Way

There's always a choice.
A new direction.
Path less trodden.
Crossroad.
Junction.
Even a U-turn requires movement.

Just make sure, wherever you're going
And whatever you do,
Just keep moving.
Even if it's in a circle
Don't stop.

You must find a way -
Over
Round
Across or through -
To leave it all behind
And discover the absolute joy
The resolute splendour of
Feeling, seeing and experiencing
Something new.
Go out on a limb
Far away from anything familiar
And not dependent on any permission from him.

How Many Times?

How many times should I forgive you?
Make allowances?
Let you get away with
Being less than I know you can be?
Ignore behaviour that isn't good?
Look the other way?
Hold back words?
Remain patient?
Turn the other cheek?
Feel grateful you're here?

Is there a number when it's okay?
A feeling to acknowledge
When humiliation can no longer be swallowed?
Lies and stories are recognised for what they are
And you've overstepped the mark once again?
What happens when enough... really is enough?
I'm only asking
Because I think I'm there –
The last straw.
The limit of my patience.
The end of my tether.
Waiting to say goodbye...
    for
        the
            very
                last
                    time.

Crossing the Line

Of course it was always there
She'd decided it years ago,
Along with expectations, boundaries
And a host of other variables
That had long since been forgotten,
As she no longer felt the need
To question your commitment
Or the depth of your love.

But still you pushed. Got complacent.
Curious. Gave into temptation.
Ruined everything. Then lied.
Even when the evidence grew
You refused to admit your part
Blamed others; eventually even her.
Despite having been caught out
Not once, but numerous times.

But I think your final undoing
Was when you asked for wriggle room.
Leeway; some reconsideration
A clean slate; to start again.
Claimed things weren't made clear
From the start, meanings were blurred.
Even questioned her own track record
And the absurd rigidity of the line.

It was only then, you realised,
That maybe you'd gone too far
And for you and her, that was it
There could be no coming back.

Prey

I tried too hard
Wanted so much
Gave everything
For what?
So, I could watch you rise.
Soar out of reach.
Exceed your potential.
Slip away from me.
To begin again
Make new memories.
Live a life that once was ours.

How quickly you have moved on.
Forgotten what I did.
The lies I told.
The sacrifices I made.
The things I ignored.
The promises we made.
The love we shared,

If I cannot rise with you,
I will fly lower.
Wait for my chance,
When your vanity
Brings you within reach.
And then with just one
Single deadly swipe,
You will once again be mine.
The hunter will have their prey.

Small c

You've taken family, friends, colleagues
Famous people and strangers too.
With steely determination, zero empathy
And no consideration for age, you have wrought havoc
Leaving only disbelief, pain and sadness in your wake.

I might not be able to halt your progress
But I refuse to capitalise you -
Allow more gravitas than you deserve.
Instead it's time to cut you down to size, lower your status
Remove some of your unjust power.

The origin of the word cancer is Greek… meaning crab.
And that's how I will now think of you;
Little,
Grouchy, sulky, irritating and bad tempered,
Scuttling off to find your next victim.

If I succeed in belittling you, perhaps I could also help to
Promote dignity, respect, self-worth, purpose and hope
Amongst those lives you have touched
And those who need, more than ever, a better outcome.

Escape

Once upon a time she wanted to explore every country,
Visit every continent
Swim in every sea
And have others testify
To how adventurous, brave and unflinching she was.

But as the years passed,
Her world shrank.
Spirit
And
Passion
Curtailed.

Instead of escaping the greyness of her life
To find unlimited beauty and
Experience sights and sounds
And cultural differences
Of foreign shores,
She accepted that no matter how far she travelled
Restlessness followed,
Swallowing her up.
Cancelling the thrill.
Leaving no space for curiosity.

Now she sits alone in her house.
Watching life pass her by.
Drawn to other people's tales
Of places she will never visit.

The relentless rain
Pounds against her window,
It's ongoing presence a strange comfort
As it silences her dreams of escape...
Forever.

decisions

Pieces

Humour

She used humour as a defence mechanism.
A shield to hide her real feelings behind.
A technique to distract, shift the focus
Away from her and her perceived shortcomings.

Everything was okay until one day
When what she had to say wasn't funny.
There was no comedic twist, gap or pun.
Which left far too many of her listeners
Shocked. Stunned.
Unavoidably stuck.
As they patiently waited to hear the punchline
That didn't come.

Good Job

It's a good job you
    Don't see the words in my head.
    Readily accept the answers I give.
    Can't understand the pain I feel.
    Accept the intricate lies I speak.
    Remain oblivious to the tells I share.

It's a good job that the words '*I'm fine*' satisfy your curiosity.
And you seem happy, untroubled and not bothered,
To find out what I really think and how I honestly feel.

I always find it such a relief
When most people take you at face value,
And remain unwilling and uninterested
To unpick the bright and brilliant illusion
You've spent your entire life constructing.

An Absolute Hoot

It was good to remake her acquaintance, see her sparkle once more.
Her appearance was a surprise, something no one could easily ignore.
Her smile lit up the room and as the stories started to flow,
People sat transfixed, no one had anywhere else to go.

They listened and they smiled, laughed until sides nearly split.
As she dazzled and beguiled, becoming a sure-fire instant hit.
Everyone moved in closer, wanting to bask in her glow,
So much to appreciate, as memories surfaced from long ago.

They clung onto every word, hoped she'd look them in the eye.
Wanting to be in her world, tap into that permanent high.
For hours they were gripped, delighted to be involved in the show,
Hoping she wouldn't leave, feeling happiness extend and grow.

But end it dutifully had to, she left as quickly as she came.
Her audience bereft, knowing nothing would be the same.
Why had she come back, because her reasons were never clear
And if they wished hard enough, would she suddenly reappear.

I miss her more than most, we've got shared history you see.
A reason to not be separated, which I'm sure you will agree,
Means I have the right to ask, make her promise to always stay,
That elusive other part of me - the better half that got away.

Obligation

Behind the beautiful veneer
Is someone I don't recognise.
Half the person she was.
Scared of living.
Lacking confidence.
Mind playing tricks.
Heart shattered into a million pieces.

I still question her decision.
Wonder why she bought the hype,
Thought love was the only answer -
And then wondered why he failed
To deliver the happiness she craved.

I tried to tell her.
Wanted her to love herself first -
Find ways to change her own life for the better
Before she simply handed over
The obligation and responsibility
To someone who clearly struggled to cope
With the enormity of their burden.

Bleak

You call it bleak, inhospitable and charmless.
Question why I chose here of all places –
Certainly different to the choice you'd have made.

But this place is my missing piece.
Everything I hoped it would be.
Its beauty is limitless
Because it lacks your footprints
Is not linked to painful memories
Does not expect an apology,
Or constantly question who I am.

And because I know you'll never visit
Just means I have yet another reason
To love it here.

Parents

They spend your teenage years worrying.
Paranoid about what you could discover.
Who you might sleep with
And what might happen as a result.
So, it's somewhat ironic
That they choose your thirties and forties
Persuading you to ignore their previous advice,
In order to give them the grandchildren
They now suddenly crave.

Shape my World

I remember the smell:
The taste
The possibilities
The colour of my dress.
Warm wine
Empty arms.
Wanting to be braver,
Invincible.
Desperately wanting to run
But with nowhere to go.

But most of all I recall you:
Inviting eyes
Tentative smile
Outstretched hand.
A fuzzy pathway of
Opportunities opening up.
You were confident
Optimistic
Oblivious to anyone else -
Apart from me.

How intoxicating:
To be your focus
Happy for you to take over
Move me forwards.
It's only now years later
As I remember every detail

That I can see it for what it was -
A pivotal moment -
Which was not only the beginning of us
But the reshaping of my world.

Like Me

She certainly looks like me.
Similar behaviours.
Almost identical mannerisms.
The way she tucks her hair behind her right ear
Is vaguely familiar.
And there is something recognisable
About the tilt of her head,
Those unflinching blue eyes
That can see right into your soul
Demanding answers, commanding attention.

But she can't be ME.
Can SHE?
Her hair is grey
Skin heavily lined
Shoulders dropping
Demeanour fading -
Quietly resigned to her fate.

I would have ignored her, but for that smile
Forcing me to remember
A time before the light faded.
When happiness came in reassuring waves
And I blossomed,
Buoyed by the
Reassurance of your love.

Because

Just because they are there
Doesn't mean I have to climb,
Swim or sail in them,
If I'm happy; allow me to appreciate
Them from afar
Let my use of them be limited.

If you want to approach them differently
That's your right.
But just because I don't enjoy,
Or want the same things as you
Doesn't put me in the wrong
Or give us cause to continually argue.

Elephant

I can forgive words said in haste.
Accusations made without facts.
Anger directed towards me,
When you feel wronged,
Are at a low ebb,
Or need to lash out.

I can forgive moments of weakness.
A need to apportion blame.
As disappointment fuels decisions,
To hurt those who
Are innocent of any crime,
Or undeserving of your lies.

I can forgive your impulsiveness.
Stories and excuses trotted out.
Vengeful actions set in motion,
On a collision course
To damage delicate bonds,
Or elicit more pain.

But whilst I can forgive you.
Excuse your emotional crimes.
I won't condone behaviours,
That made you feel
You were justified,
Or right to do what you did.

Of course, I can forgive you.
But don't ask me to forget.
Like an elephant I will remember
Every insult, allegation, nuance.
And all the times you forced me to question
My relationship with you.

Travelling Light

She never realised how little she had.
What few keepsakes there actually were.
How much she'd chosen not to collect -
Items thrown away, rather than saved.
Nothing notable or valuable.

No dependents, limited family,
Few friends and colleagues.
Funny really that all the time she was supposedly living,
She'd chosen instead to travel lightly.

Why was not important –
Until that day when leaving was the only option -
Then the speed of packing.
The absence of things and ties was critical.
Anything to help her disappear quickly
Leaving no clues as to where she was heading next.

Bannau Brycheiniog

A place worthy of two names; where grassy moorlands,
Heather-clad escarpments and old red sandstone peaks
Have been softened by weather and time.

Welcome to a diversity and richness of habitat that
Reveals green valleys, hidden lakes, cascading waterfalls,
Meandering rivers, natural caves and ancient woodlands.
Somewhere varied flora and fauna, a vibrant community –
Awash with culture and tradition –
And with a local flavour, wait to be discovered

It's a geographically rugged and challenging landscape
With dark skies and archaeological remains of others
Who have left their mark in centuries gone by.
But it's also my new home. Remote.
Inaccessible. Often abandoned. Always beautiful.
Somewhere to walk. Escape. Breath.
Not exactly a wilderness. More a place to think.
To feel. To just be.

Shielded from the humdrum of daily life
I am part of something bigger.
A single piece in a jigsaw;
Awash with history, myth and legend.
As I, a story teller in the making,
Seek to share my experiences,
Help you to see the patterns, colours and textures
Needed to bring this majestic landscape to life,
So you can be inspired by it too.

pieces

Loss

Liberated

No warning.
Time to prepare.
Just a feeling of detachment.
A loosening of ties.
Zero boundaries.
An untimely release.

As if all that had previously tethered me to the here and now
Had been disengaged.

Lost.

Leaving a blank page; a new beginning?
With nothing and no one to hold me.

I drift...

Alone.

Unsure whether to head for the reassurance
Of another safe harbour,
Or take a chance and dance in the path of the coming storm.

If Only We Knew

We never knew it wouldn't happen again,
That we'd not meet as usual.
Share stories.
Play our roles.
Tread familiar walks.
See and feel the same well practised emotions,
Which fixed us to a recognised time and place.

If we'd had an inkling that events had shifted -
The future had swerved,
Everything had changed.
Would we have done things differently?
Tried to imprint that moment
    – make it even more special
        – one last time?

This Place

It was her haven –

Somewhere calming, reassuring and familiar.
    Home to her heart.
    Testament to hard work.
    Realisation of a dream.

The changing seasons
Gave her plenty to do -
    Nature to tame.
    Space to landscape.
    Flowers to bloom.

This was her easel, her project, her life.
She was at her most comfortable here.
Put quite simply; she loved this place.

That's why it's so sad, completely unfair
Watching everything continue…
But without her there.

Loved

I can see it in your faces, patterns of loss and disbelief.
I can read it in your gestures, desolate and filled with grief.

I can hear it in your voices, sadness flowing from every pore.
I can feel it in your words, hesitant and shaken to the core.

I can sense it in your eyes, unspent tears, regret and pain.
You ask so many questions, but there's nothing left to explain

I can feel emptiness everywhere, signifying what's been lost.
A husband, father and friend, why must there be a cost?

We're lucky to have known him, felt the warmth of his care.
Urging us always forwards, joy and laughter to happily share.

But now he's been taken from us,
Leaving us strangely out of touch,
I know he'll never be forgotten,
Because he was loved so very much.

Central

Now I'm gone, don't look for me, or spend time questioning why.
Grieve, if you must, but I'd prefer it if you did two things.

Firstly, make plans for the future –
You must learn to live without me.
Take one day at a time; small steps are best.
And don't be scared to go it alone.
Whilst I'm not there by your side,
You can still carry me in your heart.

Secondly, remember.
Take pictures out of drawers.
Visit our favourite places.
Cook our best dishes.
Talk about us, things we did – the good and the bad.
See friends and let their memories feed into your own.
Recall moments of laughter.
Quiet days full of reflection.

Smile if you can - with or without tears,
Be grateful for our time,
Realise exactly what we had,
And know how lucky we were
To be at the centre of so much love.

Normality

Even though you're not here anymore
The spaces you left show no signs of shrinking.
Memories threaten to overwhelm me.
Everything I see or touch reminds me of you.
Nothing seems as good, or as fun.
The silence is too loud.
Devoid of your inane chatting or sighing,
I want something to cut through the noise,
Free me from the drowning thoughts -
Dark and suffocating -
Always waiting to claim me.

A clear-cut routine.
The reliability of normal.
An assortment of mundane tasks
Is what I cling to.
They get me through another day
Washing, cleaning, eating, walking
Even brushing my teeth
Mean I have something to mark time with,
Knowing I have achieved something,
Even if that's just counting another
   24 hours
   1440 minutes, or
   An additional 84600 seconds
          That I've spent away from you.

Lifecycle

Let me go now, release me from your grief.
I am not in the place you see before you.
I live in your stories and your pictures.
I am entwined in your thoughts and your memories
And can be conjured up whenever you need me.

Do not question the reasons for your loss,
Or wonder why everything had to change.
Death does not hold the answers,
You want or need to hear today,
As your heart and mind are still closed to the pain.

In time your questions and suffering will ease.
You will start to remember different things.
Fun and laughter, naff sayings we shared.
Family holidays, beautiful places we visited
And slowly substitute a smile for your tears.

When you are not anxiously looking for me,
As frequently or as urgently as you do now,
Please don't be sad or worried.
This does not mean you have forgotten me,
Only that the healing of loss has begun.

So, dry your eyes, I am not gone,
As long as I live in your memories
And your heart.

Memories

I can't remember what I ate yesterday,
    Or when I was supposed to pick up the dry cleaning.
I don't know the answer to that tricky pub quiz question,
    Despite the fact I saw the film recently.
I can't remember your children's names,
    Or the real story behind why you hate aubergines.
I don't know where my car keys are,
    Because I swear they move of their own accord.

But I can recall in perfect technicolour that moment
When I knew I would never see you again.
When time froze and I was faced with
The worst day of my life.
That sick feeling in my stomach...
Pain as raw today as it was 15 years ago.
Heartbreak eagerly lurking,
Waiting to claim yet another victim.
But why can I not forget these things?

Why is the past so keen I should remember?
I like to think that memories are fickle
That sometimes we need reminding
What we've faced.
How fragile everything is.
And what's important.
Just so we can congratulate ourselves
On how far we've come
And how resilient we can be.

What About Us?

What about us?
Those left behind,
Picking up the pieces,
Wavering between smiles of remembrance
And inconsolable tears of loss.

Why did it happen?
What can we do?
Where should we go?

How can we ever shift the weight of our grief,
Carry on living with some meaning
Without you to guide us,
Showing us the way.
Telling us to put one foot in front of the other,
Teaching us how to love and be loved
And explaining why we must keep going,
When giving up seems an easier option.

Why?

I know something is going on.
The balance has shifted.
I can feel the gap widening.
The numbers don't add up,
The words have stopped making sense.
Your excuses are more eloquent
Than the lies spun quickly to appease me.

As I reach out for one final embrace
- A goodbye of sorts -
My hands return empty…
You are out of reach.
My heart wrenches.
My mind whirls…
Trying to pinpoint the exact moment when the love ran out
And you thought it was easier to leave, than to tell me why.

Convenient

The kidnapped baby donkey reunited with its mum.
A litter of puppies rescued from the sewer.
The kitten nurtured by a duck.
An orphaned calf bonding with a lamb.
The dehydrated squirrel requesting a drink.
An upside-down tortoise saved by his friend.
I watch them like an innocent bystander.
Willing them along.
Rooting for success.
Desperate to see good win out.
Waiting for a happy conclusion.
Whilst all the time mindful
That the tears I openly shed
Are not for these well-orchestrated clips,
Where resilience triumphs over adversity,
But to cover up the pain and loss I still feel,
As I get used to functioning without you.

Your author

Vicky Boulton grew up in North Yorkshire. Fascinated with words, she started writing poetry when she was 10 and has no intention of stopping any time soon. She lives with her husband and several dogs, dividing her time between Northamptonshire and the Breacon Beacons.

Not for Everybody is Vicky's third anthology. Her first, *Eighty-Eight*, dealt with the joys and disappointments of relationships, love, growing up and getting older. Whilst her second, *What Will People Think?* took readers on a poetic voyage through menopause, relationships, communications and self-awareness.

Other books by Vicky Boulton

Eighty-Eight - the joys and disappointments of relationships, love, growing up and getting older. ISBN 978-1-78222-817-2

What Will People Think? - a poetic voyage through menopause, relationships, communications and self-awareness.
ISBN 978-1-78222-921-6

Milton Keynes UK
Ingram Content Group UK Ltd.
UKHW020840050624
443777UK00015B/520